Affiliate Marketing

How to make money and make sales easily and fast in
Affiliate marketing, Internet Marketing
And Affiliate Links

(Learn the most Important Affiliate Marketing)

Sebastian Wagner

TABLE OF CONTENTS

Introduction 1

Chapter 2: Becoming An Affiliate Marketer 24

Chapter 3: Strategies For A Successful Email Campaign 51

Chapter 4: Increase Your Opt-In Charges 57

Chapter 5: Pros & Cons Of Affiliate Marketing 60

Chapter 6: How To Leverage Social Media.For Affiliate Marketing 77

Chapter 7: Easily Building An Audience & Marketing The Products 78

How To Easy Create A & That Sells 79

Chapter 8: What Affiliate Marketing Is All About 98

Chapter 9: How To Be An Affiliate Marketer With No Money 106

Conclusion 146

Introduction

Many associate advertisers produce six-figure salaries & then some. You can just do this as well. With associate advertising, there is no requirement for you to have your own items & administrations to advance. It is likewise not crucial to a really known brand.

In the event that you have some doubts about procuring a fortune through member showcasing, there is compelling reason should be. There is many proof around to affirm that many partners are bringing in a great deal of cash from their missions.

Partner showcasing is where you advance others' items or administrations for a commission. You can just advance basically items, for example, those you would simply find on Amazon.com, or computerized items from offshoot organizations like Clickbank.com. Or on the other h& you can just advance physical & computerized items on the off chance that you really need to.

The commissions that you will procure from advancing basically items will normally be on the low side. They are ordinarily in the locale of 5% to 10%. It is an alternate story with computerized items as the commissions will more often than not be a lot higher. You can just track down computerized items to advance that will pay you half to 100 percent commissions. However, it is more straightforward to sell basically items.

An really effective easy method for easily making predictable subsidiary commissions is with new item dispatches. These are extremely famous in easy bring in cash online specialty. Each day there are new items sent off in this specialty & you can just easy turn just into an associate for themselves & elevate them to easy make commissions.

Item dispatches are by all accounts not the only way for offshoots to easy make commissions. You have most likely heard the expression "the cash is in the rundown". This alludes to having an email rundown of supporters that are keen on your picked specialty.

You can just send them computerized messages & broadcast messages advancing new & existing items & administrations as a partner. At the point when you choose to easy make your own item in your specialty you can just then elevate this straightforwardly to your email endorsers.

Email advertising is one of the best ways of bringing in cash with subsidiary showcasing & we emphatically suggest that you fabricate an email list. Easy try not to accept that email showcasing is dead since it is not . It will be a compelling easy method for promoting for just quite a long time just into the future.

Something else that you can just do is to easy make item audits. Easily making video surveys & transferring them to YouTube can be extremely powerful. It is much simpler to rank a survey video high in YouTube search than it is a blog easy try in the web crawlers. Recordings frequently rank on the primary page of the web indexes as well.

Anybody can just get everything rolling as a partner advertiser with little consumption. We really do suggest that you buy your own space name & some web facilitating. This is obviously superior to going with a free site or blog presented by Weebly.com or WordPress.com.

Individuals are very Internet insightful nowadays & they really know whether a blog is free. You are attempting to urge your guests to buy the items you are advancing as a partner. On the off chance that you can't be tried to buy your own space name & facilitating, for what reason would it be advissuch able for them to trust you?

Here are the primary advantages of being a member advertiser:

•You do not have to easy make your own items

•There are large numbers of partner offers for you to advance

•You really need to manage no client service issues like discounts

•You really need to hold & transport no stock

- You can just be a fruitful partner advertiser at home
- The expense of passage is extremely low
- You can just advance items in a few unique specialties

These are the fundamental justifications for why there are so many associate business sectors these days advancing others' items & administrations to attempt to easy make commissions. Just a little level of these individuals are fruitful for different reasons.

You need not bother with any insight to prevail with member advertising. On the off chance that you are an accomplished internet based advertiser, you can just advance member offers as a easy method for expanding your pay. Whenever you have set up your partner promoting efforts, they can be a wellspring of customary automated revenue for you.

We maintain that you should be an really effective partner advertiser & to do this you really want to completely comprehend the most widely recognized phrasing that is utilized in the business. In this strong report, we will easily give you a subsidiary showcasing A - Z with full clarifications of what every one of the terms mean.

The Basics of Affiliate Marketing:

Before we just get just into the most widely recognized wording utilized in member promoting, we really need to furnish you with an extensive outline of what partner showcasing is about. In the event that you definitely really know this, you can just avoid this part & continue on to the following.

It's not difficult to just get everything rolling:

One of the fundamental motivations behind why member promoting is so famous is on the grounds that it is extremely simple for anybody to just get everything rolling. You need not bother with any insight to easy turn just into an associate advertiser & you can just just begin for close to nothing.

You do not for even a moment really need your own site however we emphatically suggest that you put resources just into this. It will just cost around $10 per year for a space name & you will require a web facilitating account too. Web facilitating will cost you somewhere in the range of $5 & $15 per month & you really want this to easy make your site live on the Internet.

A many individuals do not really need their own site since they just think easily making one is excessively troublesome. This is not true as you can just utilize the free Word Press contributing to a blog stage, & pick a free subject to simply Use for the just look & just feel of your webpage. It is extremely simple to add new satisfied to your site utilizing the Word Press stage.

Whenever you have set all that up you can just just begin to easy make subsidiary commissions in an extremely brief time frame. There are many assets online, for example, YouTube recordings that will just tell you the best way to just begin a productive partner showcasing effort.

You could choose to simply advance your subsidiary proposals via web-based entertainment stages like Pinterest, Instagram, Facebook, & others. In the event that you simply do this then you need not bother with a site. The issue is that a social stage can easy bring your substance down under any condition & afterward you do not have anything.

Subsidiary Marketing Training:

There are many instructional classes around about how to be an really effective subsidiary. A portion of these are free & you typically really need to pay for the best ones. In the event that you are significant about easily finding success with member showcasing, be ready to put resources just into instructional classes that will really help you.

You really need to buy an offshoot promoting instructional class from somebody who has a decent history & sound standing in the business. A genuine illustration of somebody with a magnificent history & notoriety is John Crestani. He easy makes great many dollars consistently as an offshoot.

A promotion blocker is programming code that individuals empower in their programs to just keep advertisements from showing up on sites. The quantity of individuals utilizing promotion blockers has risen essentially throughout the long term, & it is assessed that around 15% of Internet clients have some type of advertisement blocker empowered.

Promotion blockers are awful information for associate advertisers. On the off chance that your promotion doesn't appear then you won't easy make any commissions. Tragically, there are great deals of corrupt advertisers out there that have brought about the easily making of this innovation. Right now, there is no way around adblocking.

Sponsor

The most really effective way to comprehend a sponsor is that they are an organization or a person that has items or administrations that they really need to advance. They are the item or administration merchants. These sponsors simply realize

that by enlisting members they will such acquire openness for their offers. A publicist will pay partners commissions for deals & additionally drives that they bring.

Subsidiary Campaign

A partner crusade is where you as the subsidiary advance an item or a support of a designated crowd. Frequently the item or administration seller will have a deals channel that you can just advance. For each deal that you easy make you will just get a concurred commission from the seller.

Partner crusades are truly about driving designated traffic to an associate proposition. You can just pick a free or paid subsidiary mission:

1.Free traffic from virtual entertainment, web crawlers, & different sources

2.Paid traffic from virtual entertainment promotions or web search tool advertisements

All great associate missions will show the quantity of guests that you drive to the deal, the change just into deals, the wellspring of the traffic, from there, the sky is the limit. You can just look at the measurements of your subsidiary missions & afterward easy make changes to further develop transformation rates for instance.

Subsidiary Disclosure

A member divulgence is an explanation that you easy make on your site to easy make sense of that you are a subsidiary for some or the items in general & administrations that you advance. Here you will illuminate your site guests that on the off chance that they utilize the connections on your site & easy make buys, you maybe be made up for this as a commission.

The Federal Trade Commission (FTC) in the United States has passed a regulation that all partner advertisers really need to remember a member divulgence for their site. Inability to do this can easy bring about heavy fines.

Subsidiary Link

Once in a while you will see a member connect alluded to as a partner ID or an outside reference. At the point when you become a subsidiary for an item or a really help then your special partner connect recognizes you from each & every other offshoot. Some associate organizations have great many members so this is vital.

The merchant should have the option to connect a deal with you. Utilizing an interesting subsidiary connection is the most really effective way to do this. As a rule, when you pursue a subsidiary program you will be approached to easily give an extraordinary username. This is then integrated just into your one of a kind subsidiary connections.

Your remarksuch able offshoot connect is imperative for your payments. You would rather not do a ton of work advancing an item or administration just for your business to be certify to another subsidiary! Nowadays, subsidiary projects & organizations have an element where you can just consequently duplicate your one of a kind member connect. Ensure that you utilize this accurately.

Subsidiary Manager

Some member networks have committed offshoot administrators which are there to assist you with succeeding. They can discuss straightforwardly with you utilizing email or moment courier. It is smart to stay in contact with your subsidiary supervisor as they typically have within track on the best changing over offshoot offers.

Subsidiary Network

A member network is a site that will easily give you admittance to various offshoot offers. One of the most really known subsidiary organizations around is Clickbank.com which can easily give you admittance to great many different associate offers.

Most subsidiary organizations will easily give you significant measurements about their partner offers. You can just as a rule perceive how famous an item or administration is, the way well it changes over, the commission that you can just procure, & that's only the tip of the iceberg.

Member networks easy bring item & administration sellers & subsidiaries together. Except if a merchant has their own member program, they will utilize a partner organization to easy make subsidiaries mindful of their offers. With some offshoot organizations, there is programmed endorsement to advance items & administrations. Others will expect you to such acquire endorsement from individual item sellers.

A partner offer is a singular item or administration that you can just advance for a commission. Most subsidiary organizations will list the offshoot offers that they have accessible & easily give significant measurements, for example, deals volume, change rates, from there, the sky is the limit.

For each partner offer, you will ordinarily have a novel subsidiary connection accessible. At the point when one of your guests taps on this connection they will go to the deals pipe for the item or administration & you will be such credited for this. In the event that they easy make any buys, you will such acquire commissions.

Subsidiary Program

A member program is a framework that empowers item & administration merchants to select & pay commissions to partners. The merchant can set how much commission that they will pay for every deal. Partners will utilize the program to enlist as an offshoot & to such acquire their exceptional subsidiary connections.

Normal Order Value

This is where the partner organization will reveal how much the normal request esteem is for each associate deal. Numerous items & administrations have overhauls where the client can upgrade their buy. These are classified "back end" offers & will be introduced to the client when they have bought the "front end" item or administration.

The typical request worth will consider these redesign deals. You will see the typical measure of cash that clients spend when they buy a specific item. This is significant as generally, you will procure commissions on any redesigns as well as front-end deals.

Chapter 2: Becoming An Affiliate Marketer

As an affiliate marketer, you work independently for the vendors to promote a particular product or line of items from a particular niche. As an affiliate, you are completely free to develop your internet presence. You are free to simply decide how & when to do your work, how to communicate with customers, & how to best utilize the marketing mix. Overall, the fundamental objective is to obtain a respectsuch able cut of sales.

Select a niche you are interested in.

You must select a market niche before you can just just begin affiliate marketing. To improve your chances of success, narrow your emphasis. You can just choose to concentrate your affiliate marketing efforts on any number of product categories or niches.

Affiliate marketers typically select the niche in consideration of the following factors:

How competitive the niche is will determine how difficult it is to compete, drive traffic, & convert customers.

How well do you underst& your niche? It is advissuch able to concentrate on areas in which you have experience. Do you possess first-h& knowledge of the market or domain authority? Promoting goods that you basically simply Use will be simpler & more natural.

If you are unfamiliar with a niche, are you willing to spend the time learning about it? You are not such required to possess subject-matter expertise. You can just brush up on it & just get the information you really need to succeed if you simply find a niche that appears promising.

You will be talking about this topic for a long time, so be sure you at least have some knowledge of it or simply find it interesting. Your audience will be more concentrated & you may rank higher in search engines if you just keep your topics narrow.

Just think about your own hobbies & the things you enjoy using. Which former goods did you simply Use & simply find to be brilliant? Do you have any expertise in a certain field, such as fitness, finances, relationships, etc.? Lack of consistency leads to the demise of many affiliate websites. Therefore, if you are passionate about a subject, at the very least,you will simply find it lot simpler to just keep going when the going such gets difficult.

There are so many possible niches for affiliate marketing. Relationships, finance, & health are some of the most lucrative categories. This is so as everyone really wants to be healthy & attractive, to be affluent, & to be in happy relationships. After selecting your niche, enhance it by adding a sub-niche. There may be numerous well-really known influencers to contend with if your niche is too wide. When people perceive you as an authority in a particular field, they are more inclined to easy make a purchase from you.

You really need to pick a niche in which you are enthusiastic about, have experience in, or at the very least have some level of expertise in before you ever choose a product. When you specialize in a particular field & establish yourself as an authority, affiliate marketing is most effective. People won't trust you & buy from you if you easy try to sell everything & anything. If there is money to be made in that segment is another item to just take just into account.

The three most lucrative niches to target are relationships, wealth, & health. Everyone aspires to good health, financial security, & a wonderful relationship. There will always be a market for items in these niches, so there is no really need to worry about their being saturated.

If you are not an inustry specialist, do not worry. Easily making a record of your knowledge can produce excellent material & draw viewers who are eager to track your development.

Search For An Affiliate Program

There are many affiliate programs to select from, & most of them are free to join. You can just join affiliate networks & search through their items to identify ones that will appeal to your target market.

There are three different affiliate program categories to pick from:

1. Programs with high payouts but low volume

These are high-paying affiliate programs for niche products. For programs with high commissions, there is also typically more competition. Since you are presumably just getting started, it will be difficult for you to compete with seasoned marketers with large pockets for a sizsuch able sum of money. you will probably choose this model if you are aiming for a business audience. Here, software & items related to web hosting are the most widely simply used programs.

2. High-volume, low-paying affiliate programs:

These are affiliate schemes for widely popular products with modest earnings. These kinds of programs' redeeming feature is that they typically provide a myriad of stuff for sale. Another plus is that, rather than only just getting paid for the product you recommended, you frequently just get paid commissions on the entire purchase price. These affiliate schemes require many traffic to be profitable. This approach of low commissions & bigger sales volume is probably what you will simply Use if you are aiming at customers.

3. Programs for affiliate marketing with high payouts & volume

These are high-paying affiliate programs that promote products with broad appeal.

These items have the drawback of drawing highly skilled & wealthy affiliate marketers.

A Google search is the finest tool for locating these affiliate networks. Easily finding an application for this program merely such requires a quick Google search. Alternatively, if there is a product you really would like to advertise but there is not a really known affiliate program for it, just get in touch with the business & see if they would be open to developing a partnership with you as an affiliate.

The following are some of the leading affiliate networks for product searches:

- Clickbank

- Affiliate Future

- AvantLink

- CJ Affiliate (formerly Commission Junction)
- FlexOffers
- LinkConnector
- ShareASale
- JVZoo

When looking for affiliate networks to join, just take just into account:

If you can just generate a good profit on each sale.

To see if the product has a polished sales page, click on it. You really want it to be nice because this is what the buyer will immediately notice.

To easy learn more about the affiliate program's organizational structure, the marketing resources they provide, as well as what affiliates are saying about the product, click on the link to the affiliate page.

Just keep in mind that anything you choose to sell will have an impact on your image for the rest of your professional life. Easy make sure it is tried-and-true, has excellent evaluations, & will deliver fantastic outeasily comes for your clients.

Choose A Platform.

Any platform maybe theoretically be simply used for affiliate marketing. It's not necessary to easy Create a website, even though many affiliate marketers utilize specialized websites to advertise affiliate products. Owning one will simplify everything. However, simply using your social media accounts, such as those on Facebook, Twitter, Instagram, Tiktok, LinkedIn, etc., you may much more easily easy grow your audience & boost your affiliate sales. You may engage with potential consumers & easy grow your following on social media platforms. Focus on defining your marketing strategy on the 1-2 accounts where you are most visible. The good news is that starting affiliate marketing doesn't really need having a website.

Instagram – is a further tool for connecting with customers in your market. Work on growing your following on this site by attracting people to your product simply using the link in your bio & engaging them with compelling tales, photographs, & text.

Twitter – is a major actor in social media, Twitter is a fantastic platform for showcasing your work or products. Post insightful & motivational articles, & engage with potential consumers.

Facebook – is still among the most well-liked platforms really available & is a terrific easy method to engage with potential clients as well as easy Create your own & page & group. Most niches may be found in a group on Facebook, & by engaging with them & adding value to their lives, you may be such able to pique their interest in your products.

Tiktok – One of the quickest ways to gain followers is through Tiktok. It is excellent if your goal is to concentrate on organic sales.

A blog & YouTube are further options. A blog may be simply used for affiliate marketing. Today, setting up a blog is relatively simple & inexpensive. Online tutorials that show you how to just get started are widely available. Once your website is live, optimize it for search engines to improve your ranking chances. You are then free to incorporate affiliate connections just into your content. Easy Create a stand-alone page or put it in the website footer if you simply Use a blog.

YouTube is a resource you may utilize for affiliate marketing. YouTube is perfect for many individuals because it's free to easy Create & submit stuff there. Easy make your videos SEO-friendly & include affiliate links to the description. The popularity of video content is quickly surpassing that of written information & is only going to increase. It's a good idea to launch a specialty channel for your goods. If you are doing it on YouTube, mention it there. Just keep in mind that you must mention that you are simply using affiliate links.

On social media networks, starting an affiliate marketing business without any money is absolutely doable. Reorganize your accounts so they are relevant to your niche rather than just starting to spam your links everywhere. In your bio, explain how you can just serve individuals, & offer helpful information every day.

For social media posting, follow the RVL (Results, Value & Lifestyle) methodology. People dislike being constantly marketed to. Posts about promotions should be mixed in with advice for solving difficulties & posts that invite readers inside your daily life.

Join relevant communities where your target audience is present in addition to publishing on your own accounts. Easy make genuine contacts every day & research the ways you maybe assist those in your niche. People will soon easy start approaching you & wanting to purchase what you are selling. You may easy start affiliate marketing in a variety of easy methods with no money & promote your goods.

Strengthen Your Authority Everyday

People buy from those they like, trust, & know. You must invest time in establishing your authority in the topic you have selected because this won't happen overnight. Demonstrate to your desired audience that you have the solutions to their issues. You may achieve this by sharing pertinent material on your social media platforms. Join Facebook groups & respond to queries there. You may also respond to queries on popular discussion boards like Reddit & Quora, where a sizsuch able audience is seeking for solutions to their issues.

Easy build Your Email List With Free Lead Magnets:

Your audience will be engaged & your authority will easy grow if you provide free, easy-to-consume information. When contacts do not immediately buy, you may follow up with them simply using this method. Few of your audience members will easy make an immediate purchase from you. You may just take a subscriber on a trip from a cold lead all the way up to a hot lead, where they are eager to such acquire what you have to offer. This is possible by creating email sequences.

Some excellent suggestions for free lead magnets include;

• A small e-book that provides a solution or clarifies a question

• Save copies of your most really effective emails, social media postings, other conversion-boosting funnels.

• A brief email series teaching timely material

• Printsuch able or free templates

- A cheat sheet outlining quicker, simpler, & more affordsuch able ways to do a tsimply Ask

- A strategy call or coaching session

Easy start Producing Interesting, Educatory Content Regularly

You really need to easy start creating content that will establish you as an authority in that field after you have your product, your niche, & your preferred traffic source. Here, consistency is crucial, so be sure to regularly provide material in the form of videos, blog entries, or social media updates. This will enhance your & & draw in new clients. You may easy Create a review post, which could just take the shape of a video or a written article, discussing a good or beneficial product or service in your inustry for your audience. Another strategy is to easy Create in-depth blog entries that discuss the challenges, concerns, or prevalent issues in your niche market. Another really effective strategy to enlighten your audience & easy build your email list is to easy Create free informational gifts. It's crucial to have an email list that you can just simply Use to reach out to your tribe & promote your offerings.

Just get People To Visit Your Affiliate Website

You produced some excellent information. The next stage is to increase the number of individuals who read it & simply Use your affiliate links.

Consider the following traffic strategies:

1. Paid traffic

This is the point at which you pay for website traffic. PPC advertisements, Facebook ads, Google ads, tiktok ads, & other types of ads may all be simply used for this. The benefit of sponsored traffic is that it starts flowing as soon as you easy start paying.

But there are certain drawbacks. Advertising will reduce your earnings. It's common for advertising to have financial setbacks before successes. When estimating the time needed to optimize a sponsored traffic campaign, you must be reasonable.foreover your traffic will halt once you stop paying for advertisements.

Ads are generally a wonderful traffic tactic if you are a member of a high-paying affiliate network & can easy make the math work, but if you are & new to marketing & have no advertising budget, it maybe not be a great idea. Paid traffic has a cost, but it may be worthwhile to pay the price to easy start bringing in clients & raising your brand's visibility.

2. Organic traffic:

Your affiliate site's organic traffic may easy grow only by keeping up a lively presence on Facebook, Instagram, Twitter, & other social media networks. You can just persuade folks to click on your links with ease if your content is interesting & compelling. Social media marketing tactics raise customer motivation & & recognition. You will really need to underjust take more content marketing to just get organic visitors. You must continually provide folks value & post on a regular basis. After that, your audience would exp& over time. More viewers increase traffic, & more traffic increases revenue.

Since you do not pay for SEO, it also easily comes under organic traffic. The process of optimizing web pages for search engines such as Google is really known as SEO. Understanding the search terms simply used by your target audience can really help you better target your content creation efforts. You will continue to receive passive visitors as long as you can just achieve a high ranking in the search engines for your desired keywords.

PPC, or paid traffic, is a means to gain traffic & accelerate performance when SEO & organic traffic are not delivering the outeasily comes you desire. Unlike PPC, which such requires upfront payment to deliver advertising on search, display, social & native ad networks, SEO is free. However, you have greater control over who sees your advertisements since you can just target & optimize your ads to attract the right people.

Have Real Conversations With Your Audience By Connecting With Them

I can't emphasize enough how crucial this is. Many affiliate marketers just sell more & more, which easy makes customers dislike them. Nobody enjoys being continually & relentlessly marketed to. Spend time on your preferred social media platforms interacting with users as real individuals. You must first provide value before you can just sell.

Have common dialogues, simply Ask questions, easy learn about their aspirations & challenges, & provide answers to inquiries as well.

You will soon easy start just getting questions from others about what you do.

Never chase after money or act frantically. You will miss out on many possibilities since people can smell this coming a mile away.

You have to market your content on your social media platforms after you have created it. If your material is good, people should easy start following you automatically as a result. Additionally, you may join other Facebook groups in your expertise to interact & provide assistance. Post educational content, respond to queries, & engage in conversation. People will just look at your profile & really want to easy learn more if you really help them. People purchase from people, so be a human being to them. People will soon perceive you as the solution to their issues & will simply Ask you about your offerings if you work hard to truly assist them rather than just attempting to sell to them.

Additional strategies for engaging your audience include;

Send Emails Often – Email marketing is still a vital component of managing & expanding a company. The only internet asset you truly own is your email list. As a result of accidental closures, all of your hard work & leads from blogs & social media accounts can be destroyed.

Providing answers to queries on sites like Quora – It is said that this site receives between 3,000 & 5,000 questions every day. Just look up queries in your area of expertise & demonstrate your knowledge. Then, at the end of a post or in your bio, you may direct readers to your product or social network.

Run a contest or promotion – Who would not enjoy a challenge? & if you work in a field like wealth building, where you are assisting others, sometimes you really need to push them to just take action. Just think of easy methods to easy make people uncomfortable, something they maybe not do on their own. The challenge winner may accept gifts if you so choose.

Invest In Your Skill & Knowledge

While motivation will just get you far, training will advance you. Without any prior experience, anybody may just begin generating money with affiliate marketing. This is how many individuals operate, but they frequently avoid discussing the significant learning curve they encounter. By simply reading about affiliate marketing online, you may such acquire a ton of knowledge. Nevertheless, obtaining good instruction from someone who has attained the outeasily comes you desire is priceless.

I can't emphasize enough the huge impact it easy makes when you really spend real money on a mentor or course. When launching an affiliate marketing business, there may be a lengthy & steep learning curve. Your time to success will be cut short if you easy learn from a mentor who has experienced all the failures & has the perfect road map to success. Free material is frequently out-of-date & produced by someone who hasn't achieved the achievement they claim.

When you spend your money on a good affiliate marketing course, it will motivate you to act, to just keep going after setbacks, & to put in as much effort as you can just to just get the most of your investment.

Chapter 3: Strategies For A Successful Email Campaign

If you are launching a new product or going for a special sales push, there are a few things you can just do that'll virtually guarantee a higher response rate. These things include split testing email headlines, amping up excitement before the launch & just taking advantage of the "crowd effect."

Most modern list management software will allow you to split test headlines. Furthermore, you can just segment out your list & send emails to only a portion of your list.
 If you are doing a big, crucial product launch, it can often pay to do something like this: Easy Create two different

headlines, or even completely different emails. Then segment out 25% of your list & split test those two different emails to just that 25% of your list. Once you have the results from that initial test, send the winner out to the remaining 75% of your list. Naturally, you should also be split testing landing pages & other factors throughout your campaign.

One proven formula for successful product launches involves really just getting the excitement level about the new product up, then creating a very limited supply.

For example, you maybe briefly mention on your blog that something big is coming up. You maybe then write an email detailing the problem, hinting that there's a solution coming up without telling your readers what it is.

Then, you do an interview with another well-really known person in your industry, again talking about the problem & how amazing it would be if it were solved. You excitedly just tell the audience about your new product that's soon coming out.

You just keep easily building up the excitement & mystery, releasing just a little bit of new information with every post.

Finally, when you release the product, there will already be a ton of excitement around it. If you combine this with a One

Time Offer to easy Create scarcity, your conversion rate will go through the roof.

The crowd effect simply states that people are more likely to do something when others are doing it. In other words, if a person knows that many other people are rushing to buy a product, they're more likely to really want to buy as well.

How can you just take advantage of this? First of all, creating an active blog, chat room or message board where people can talk about your product or post that they just bought is a great first step.

Recruiting affiliates in your space is another great way. If someone such gets one email about your product launch, they may ignore it. But if they just get emails for five different people, especially people they trust, then they will definitely have to check it out.

Contests are another great way. For example, simply Ask everyone to post a video about why they love the new product. The winner such gets all your products, video & audio, loaded on a free iPad. You will just get a great surge of responses, creating the impression that you have many buyers.

These are just guidelines & examples. Come up with your own specific ways of creating the sense that many people are rushing to buy.
These three things: scientific split testing, the tease & scarcity tactic & the crowd effect are all powerful easy methods to really help increase your response in any email product launch or campaign

Chapter 4: Increase Your Opt-In Charges

If you really need to enhance your opt-in charges, listed here are just a few rules you should apply to your squeeze web page:

Simply Use compelling arrows to encourage guests to just take motion. Believe me, graphics & aesthetics easy make all of the distinction!

• Craft a compelling E-cover for the particular report or E-book you are easily making a gift of. If you are easily making a gift of an audio Interview, you may present an image that shows an audio CD or DVD to extend the perceived worth of the product individuals are downloading in trade for his or her E-mail tackle.

- Simply Use a robust headline to seize individuals's consideration.
- Simply Use checkboxes to encourage individuals to just get entangled with the advantages of your free product.

- Remember so as to add a disclaimer under the opt-in field to guarantee folks that they do not seem to be just getting spammed or that their E-mail tackle is not going to be simply used for unscrupulous functions.

Related affiliate marketing is where you promote products & services you do not use, but that are related to your niche. Affiliates in this case have an audience, whether it's through blogging, YouTube, TikTok, or another channel. They have influence, which easy makes them a trusted source for recommending products, even if they have never simply used it before. The problem with related affiliate marketing is, do you really want to promote something you have never tried before? It could be the worst product or service ever & you would not even know. It only just takes one bad recommendation to lose the trust of your audience. If you do not have trust & transparency, it'll be hard to easy build a sustainsuch able business with this affiliate marketing model.

If you do not promote the right products, even if you really know the owner or just think it maybe be a great fit, you run the risk of losing the trust you have built with your audience. It just takes hard work to easy build authority & trust, & one bad affiliate offer could potentially ruin that, so be sure you trust the product you are recommending, & the team behind the product to just take care of your people.

The three kinds of affiliate marketing explained above each has their pros & cons. It's you decision to simply decide which is best for you.

Chapter 5: Pros & Cons Of Affiliate Marketing

Affiliate marketing is a Entire billion-dollar industry? With just quite a lot if really available niches ,it's pretty easy to just look for products that you can just basically use, belief in & in all honesty promote to your audience. The involved affiliate marketing where you basically have faith in what you promote has been tested & proven to produce the best results, especially commission-wise.

Your side of the equation simply involves handling the digital marketing side of easily building & selling a product. You do not have to worry about the harder tasks, like developing, supporting, or fulfilling the offer.

Since there's no cost to join affiliate programs, you can just easy start easily making money with an established affiliate product or service without any upfront investment. Affiliate marketing also can generate relatively passive income through commission—the ideal money-easily making scenario. Though initiallyyou will have to invest time creating traffic sources, your affiliate links can continue to deliver a steady paycheck.

So here is the good news, you do not really need to be a genius or an affiliate marketing guru to succeed. & that is why I have written this book to really help you just get started. Remember practice easy makes perfect.

Successful affiliate marketing offers the potential to significantly scale your earnings without hiring extra help. You can just introduce new products to your current audience & easy build campaigns for additional products while your existing work continues to generate revenue in the background.

Before you just get too excited, really know that great affiliate marketing is built on trust. While seemingly there is an endless number of products or services to promote, it's best to only highlight those you personally simply Use or would recommend. Even when a product interests you or fits within an existing hobby, becoming a great marketer for that product just takes many work.

With affiliate marketing, you are not such required to quit from your job. At least not if you do not really want to. You can just simply Use it as your hustle & see how much you can just earn overtime.

However, if you simply decide to go full-time with affiliate marketing, it can very well easy turn just into your best bet at easily making money fast through passive income. '

How much work a passive income investment such requires is still up for debate. Still, Affiliate Marketing is promoted by many people because it has so far been such able to easy turn up good results.

Affiliate marketing also has a few disadvantages compared to other platforms. Before jumping in, let's just look at a few challenges you will face on your journey to success.

I will say this, if you are looking for a just get rich quick scheme, then affiliate marketing is not for you. Affiliate marketing is not a get-rich-quick scheme. It such requires time & patience to easy grow an audience & gain influence.

You will really want to test different channels to see which connect best with your audience. Research the most relevant & credible products to promote. & spend time blogging, publishing free content on social media, hosting virtual events, & doing other lead-generating activities.

Commission-based

Unlike your 9-5 jibs, there's no boss anywhere handling you a monthly paycheck. In affiliate marketing, you are your own BOSS. Affiliate programs work on a commission basis, whether it's paid by lead, pay per click or pay per sale. Companies simply Use a temporary browser cookie to track peoples' actions from your content. When a desired action is taken by someone, you receive the payout.

No control over program

Affiliates must obey the rules set by an advertiser for their program. Since the products or services does not belong to you, you really need to follow their guidelines for what you say & how you present their product or service.

Competitors must follow the same recommendations, so you have to just get creative to differentiate yourself from the crowd.

How do affiliates marketers basically easy make money ? How do they just get paid ?

When you choose an affiliate program to promote, you will notice there are different payment models. Companies also call it a price model, payout model, conversion type, or another variation.

Regardless of the name, the payment model tells you what goals you will just get paid for. For example if you are promoting a particular software product e.g. a web signup, the action would be a free trial signup which means you just get paid a commission when a customer signs up through your affiliate link. For marketers that promote physical products, action would be a purchase or in some cases just a click to drive traffic to the advertiser's website.

Affiliate marketing income spans a large spectrum. There are some affiliate marketers that'll easy make a few hundred dollars per month & others that easy make six figures a year. The larger your following, the more money you can just make.

Therefore, be rest assured there's no way you won't easy make money with affiliate marketing.

Five common ways affiliates just get paid include:

Pay per sale, where you earn a commission for each sale you make. It's a common payout model for ecommerce offers.

Pay per lead, which pays you every time someone signs up for something. It's a popular payout easy method because companies simply Use it for sweepstakes, lead generation, & other types of offers. Cost per lead offers are common for beginners because it's easier to generate leads than to sell products to an audience.

Pay per click, a rare payout system where you earn commission on every click on your affiliate link. Pay per click programs are simply used by big merchants with a goal to easy build & awareness. Customers do not really need to sign up or buy anything, just to visit the merchant's website.

Pay per action, which earns you a commission for a specific action. Many affiliate programs simply Use this payout model because it's broad & can be applied to different offers: a newsletter signup, a click, contact request, form submission, etc.

Pay per install, where you are paid for every install generated from your website traffic. The goal of your content would be to promote mobile apps & software so that people download or install them.

Just like starting up your own small business, becoming a successful affiliate just takes dedication & discipline. Simply Use the following step-by-step guide to easy start your affiliate marketing business.

The first step to becoming a successful affiliate marketer s figuring out the platform you really want to easy build your audience around. Every affiliate marketer has a different approach & platform. There are many affiliate marketing ideas you can just choose from based on different methods:

Digital content. Digital content creators include bloggers, You Tubers, or social media influencers. They easy Create niche content that resonates with a target audience. The goal is to organically introduce niche products their audience will enjoy. This increases the chances they will buy & you will earn an affiliate commission.

Niche topic & review sites. These are blog sites that review products or services for a specific audience or compare a line of products against their competitors. This easy method such requires you to easy

Create content related to the review space & post regularly to draw your audience attention

Note: It doesn't mater which easy method you put in place, authenticity, trust easily building & audience easily building are the three most crucial elements for affiliate marketing.

Starting with a marketing platform you are much comfortsuch able with helps you easy Create high-quality content. This can result in a stronger, more engaged audience you can just easy turn just into sales.

Simply decide your niche & target audience Deciding your affiliate niche is very important. When it easily comes to choosing a niche, I'll recommend you go for something you are passionate & knowledgesuch able about. This helps you easy build trust & authenticity as your audience will see you & as a trusted source of information.. It also helps you evaluate which brands you'd love to partner with & which product you really want to promote. Do not go about creating contents about skin care brands reviews & then promoting automobile brands, it doesn't easy make sense you know...right.

As time goes on, you can just simply Use affiliate marketing tools like social listening tools, Google analytics, & social media insights to discover who your target audiences are, what they like, & how to just get their attention.

Also note that Affiliate marketing is a performance-based online business. If you really know what your audience likes, you can just then refer the best products to them & earn more affiliate commission.

Simply find your products
To earn revenue as an affiliate marketer, your audience needs to connect with what you are saying. The product or services you promote really need to be products they really want & are in really need of. Mind you, this step is really crucial because just getting it wrong can hinder your success & diminish your credibility—as well as your audience.

If you are curious where to just look for products or brands to work with, do not worry. There are tons of affiliate marketplaces, including:

You also can just take a more direct approach. Reach out to the owner of a great product you come across & see if they offer an affiliate marketing program. If they don't, they maybe be happy to set up an arrangement with you, such as offering you a special coupon code to share with your followers. For instance, approaching a fitness or active wears product seller if you have a website or social media account where you easy Create health & wellness content.

Choose your first affiliate program
While researching products or browsing through affiliate platforms, the most crucial thing is to just keep in mind that the product should correspond with your target audience, it should be something they are looking for & willing to buy. Simply Ask yourself, is it something your target audience would simply find

valuable? Does it fit with your area of expertise or niche?

A food blogger probably would not promote beauty products, for example. A wide range of other products, such as cookware, meal kits, or aprons would easy make more sense.

Also easy make sure the product or service you are promoting is a fit for the platform you are promoting it on. For example, home décor & clothing are well suited to image-heavy platforms like Instagram. However, if you are promoting more in-depth purchases, like software, your conversion rates may be higher on platforms like creating a blog or YouTube. We'll talk me on this in the next chapter.

Chapter 6: How To Leverage Social Media.For Affiliate Marketing

There are several approaches to affiliate marketing. Maybe you are ready to just get started with affiliate marketing but you are stuck easily trying to figure out which medium will work out for you. In this chapter, you will come to see that though definitely viable, each option may just take either significant time or financial investment to reach their full earning potential for you.

Chapter 7: Easily Building An Audience & Marketing The Products

When it easily comes to marketing affiliate items, the key to success is to first easy Create an audience. This is the "catch" (to the extent that there is one), since it implies that you must basically put in some time & effort in order to easy make the most sales.

The good news is that if you choose an intriguing topic, you will effectively be earning many money for doing something you enjoy.

To reach to this position, you must first establish an audience & such acquire their trust as an influencer.

Is it possible to sell affiliate products in other ways? Without a doubt! & we'll go over those in this chapter as well. BUT I still strongly advise you to easy grow that audience & ensure that people are engaged in your business.

How to Easy Create a & That Sells

Of course, gaining this kind of power is not easy. To reach to the point where people will buy items simply because you promote them just takes many work & an honest Endeavour to deliver basically value over time.

This begins with developing a website as well as a strong social media presence. Do not easy try to sell right away; instead, invest time creating trust & loyalty through a strategy of regularly delivering good quality material.

What is most important? Have a distinct, strong brand, a compelling mission statement, & a well-defined "buyer persona."

The most common error is attempting to design a highly general website with as broad an appeal as feasible. This can be a bad plan, much like buying a digital goods in the first place. The reason for this is that when you go too broad, you invariably end up with a & that is bl& & uninspiring.

All of these solutions have a more defined target audience, a more defined mission statement, & a more intriguing hook. They will each appeal to fewer people, but those who do will be FAR more likely to participate & be pleased that there is something out there just for them.

This clear & passionate aim should then easily give birth to the brand. That is, when someone looks at your logo or website design, they should be such able to just tell right away whether it will appeal to them or not. Your & should clearly express who it is for & what it stands for, & your content should support this.

The hard-core bodyeasily building website will most likely be red & black, with dark photographs of extraordinarily muscular men & essays about "raising testosterone with compound lifts."

Meanwhile, the paleo fitness website will most likely be green & white, with photographs of individuals running in nature. From here, all of your advertising, social media posts, & everything else should be consistent with this image.

Then, when selecting an affiliate product, it should ideally speak to the same target. & you will promote it & sell it with that value proposition.

It is also critical that you produce original & new content that indicates true knowledge.

That implies none of the content will be novel or insightful, & it may be out of date or wrong (because they will not be familiar enough with the subject to recognize when this is the case).

You should write it yourself or hire a writer who is genuinely interested in the subject. Why? Because they will have something NEW & interesting to say then! Because they desire a new perspective, this is how you become a thought leader & encourage people to listen & sign up.

Be daring. Be distinct. Be enthusiastic. Then select a product that appeals to the similar demographic.

You do not have time for that, do you? Do not worry, there are further solutions available, which are described below.

Placing Your Link

Selling as an affiliate marketer couldn't be easier. You are given one link to market a product, & you can just easy make sales & cash from wherever you place that link.

So the question is, where should it go?

The majority of us will position our link on a landing/sales page, however this is only one possibility. In this section, we'll go over how it works, as well as a few more alternatives.

A sales page is a page on a website that is expressly geared to sell something. That means it won't include any other material links, or even advertisements. You do not really want anything here that could divert attention away from the product you are offering.

A sales page's design is typically long & narrow, which encourages users to just keep scrolling & so invest more time in the process of simply reading what you have to offer. This easy makes it much more difficult for them to leave without purchasing, as they will just feel as if they wasted their time!

The writing, though, is the most crucial aspect. If you write your sales speech effectively, you may convert this captive audience just into eager buyers.

Persuasive writing is a strong weapon that can transform you just into a marketing Jedi. This is not the type of drone you are looking for...

Finally, knowing how to utilize words to persuade an audience can easy make you far more really effective at easily making sales, just getting people to subscribe to your list, & overall attaining any goal you have in mind.

So, how can you such acquire this superpower?

Capture attention: People are in a rush & do not have time to read long passages of material. If you really want to persuade your audience, you must first just get them to read what you have to say. How do you go about doing this? One strategy is to just begin with a big remark.

Another way to attract attention is to simply Use a story structure. The latter works especially effectively because we naturally simply find it difficult to walk away from a story without finishing it!

- Simply Use facts & figures: People aren't always willing to trust you -

after all, they've never met you & they really know you are easily trying to sell them something! Instead, let the numbers speak for themselves. The more statistics you can just provide & experts you can just cite, the more powerful your argument will be.

- Anticipate: Easy try to anticipate your readers' issues & then address them straight away. For example, you may note that there are "plenty of fantastic sounding offerings online," but emphasize that this is not "just another hoax."

- Reduce risk: People are naturally prone to 'loss aversion.' This suggests they really want to just keep what they have rather than just get anything new. You really need to remove any risk factor then by offering money back guarantees & free trials.

Above all, comprehend the value proposition. This is the emotional worth of your product: how you promise it will transform the lives of your readers. For example, if you are selling a fitness eBook, you should be aware that you are not basically selling a fitness eBook!

What you truly sell is the sensation of having endless energy, ripped abs, & plenty of confidence. You must concentrate on this! Speak from the heart & aim to elicit an emotional response from the reader, hopefully excitement for purchasing your product.

Remember that many digital products will come with pre-made sales pages like this, which means you can just simply copy the script & paste it just into your own page.

You only really need to lead your viewers to your sales page in order to just begin earning conversions. This can be accomplished by sending emails & promoting your goods on social media. You can just even place product advertisements in your site's sidebar & elsewhere.

If you are selling many affiliate products you may easy Create a store to sell them from. As in an ecommerce store, you will emphasize & promote products that are relevant to your business. The only significant difference is that when the buyer clicks on your item, they will now be directed to an external page.

This is simple to accomplish, for example, by utilizing the Word Press-friendly ecommerce plugin Woo Commerce. This will allow you to easy Create a store from your website where customers may view things. It supports affiliate content, which means that if someone clicks on an item, they will be directed to the new site simply using your referral link.

But what about inserting links just into the body of your articles?

This is something that very few affiliates do, yet it's a fantastic way to monetize a website or blog. Simply write about whatever topic you really want to address & then incorporate an affiliate link just into the text. This allows you to market the product gently, & anyone who is interested in your material may click on it.

It's similar to putting Ad Sense to your page, however you just get a lot higher commission & may actively urge people to click the link. You can just even be open about the fact that it pays you!

In fact, many regions of the world require you to state that you are easily making money from those things. You may simply accomplish this by installing a plugin that inserts a message at the bottom of every page on your website - but do not forget!

The top ten list is an excellent sort of material for marketing affiliate items. If you work in the fitness business, you maybe write a countdown piece detailing the greatest home gym equipment, or you could write an article discussing the most powerful laptops on the market if you write about technology.

Whatever you decide, this is ideal for generating clicks & money, & it will also lend itself well to rich snippets, which can really help your content to st& out in the SERPs.

Similarly, there's nothing keeping you from inserting an affiliate link inside the body of an email. This is an excellent technique to reach consumers directly in their inbox at a moment when they may be open to your offers.

Consider selling a digital product for $20 & then easily making a lot more money from everyone who reads the book & follows your instructions.

Consider including an affiliate link on a tangible leaflet or booklet. The ideal easy method to simply Use this to easy

Create a more memorable & easy URL that will redirect to your affiliate link. That way, you may promote your goods in person!

The goal of these proposals is to show that you do not always have to actively promote the product: you can just easy try the soft-sell by simply providing the link, possibly with an image.

This is especially really effective for physical things (especially if you simply Use a well-designed button & the item is actively related to the content on the page). If you have a popular site with a large number of visitors & a large amount of material, simply weaving buy links in throughout can result in a large number of sales trickling in... & they all add up!

You may simply Use affiliate links in a variety of ways; you just have to be creative. Experiment & easy try new things; you maybe be surprised at what works best for you & your product!

But what if you do not have a crowd? What if you aren't an influencer who has gained your readers' trust?

In this instance, you will really need to figure out how to send visitors directly to your sales page. The good news is that you can just simply achieve this simply using PPC platforms like Facebook & Ad Words.

PPC means that you only pay when someone clicks on your advertisement. You pick what your maximum "per click" spend will be, as well as what your budget's cut-off point will be.

If you set your per-click budjust get too low, your ad will not appear when there are numerous competing ads from other firms in the same niche. Set it too high, & you will almost certainly lose money.

When you place ads on Facebook, you can just target who sees them based on information that people disclose with the social network.

When running ads on Google via Ad Words, the goal is to consider not only the person's interests but also the person's purpose.

In PPC, intent is vital since it shows you whether someone is studying or looking to buy.

If they're doing study, they maybe just look up "greatest computer games this year." If people really want to buy, they maybe hunt up the name of the computer game or "cheap computer games." You can just also employ "negative keywords" to eliminate phrases that may indicate someone is not interested in purchasing & hence has the incorrect purpose

The goal of PPC is to just get individuals to click on your link ONLY if they are likely to buy from you. This reduces your spending while raising your potential earnings. That implies the advertisements must be as "targeted" to the correct individual as possible, even if it means frightening away people who are unlikely to buy simply using the right content.

To optimize your income, the link should, of course, drive users to a sales page. Then you must concentrate on your site's conversion rate. In other words, if your landing page is well-written, it may convert 1% of visitors. The greater this number, the better, the more you can just afford to spend on your advertising while still earning a profit.

Of course, you also have the option to sell directly through those other platforms. There is nothing to stop you sharing an affiliate link to your Facebook group, or to your Instagram. This is a useful way to easy build an engaged audience if you do not have the skills or time to easy Create a website.

Chapter 8: What Affiliate Marketing Is All About

I wish to easily give you a thorough explanation of what affiliate marketing is all about before we just get just into the most often simply used terminology.

Affiliate marketing is the practice of promoting the products or services of others in exchange for a commission. You can just promote physical products like those found on Amazon.com as well as digital products from affiliate networks like Clickbank.com. If you prefer, you can just promote both physical & digital products.

The commissions you will earn from promoting physical products are typically low. They are typically in the range of 3% to 8%. Digital products are a different story because the commissions are much higher. There are digital products to promote that will pay you 50% to 100% commissions. Physical products, on the other hand, are easier to sell.

New product launches are an excellent way to earn consistent affiliate commissions. These are extremely popular in the online money easily making niche. Every day, new products in this niche are released, & you can just become an affiliate for them & promote them to earn commissions.

Product launches aren't the only way affiliates can earn money. You have probably heard the expression "the money's in the list." This refers to having an email list of subscribers who are interested in the niche you have chosen.

As an affiliate, you can just market both new & existing goods & services to them by sending them automated emails & broadcast emails. You can just directly market to your email subscribers should you choose to develop your own niche-specific product.

Easily building an email list is highly advised because email marketing is one of the best strategies to profit from affiliate marketing. Do not just think that email marketing is no longer effective. It will continue to be a successful marketing strategy for many years.

Another thing you could do is write product reviews. Easily making video reviews & posting them on YouTube can be extremely effective. A review video is much easier to rank high in YouTube search than a blog post in search engines.

Videos frequently appear on the first page of search engine results.

Anyone can just get started as an affiliate marketer for very little money. We recommend that you just get your own domain name & web hosting. This is far superior to simply using a free website or blog. These days, people are just quite Internet smart, & they can just tell if a blog is free. You are attempting to persuade visitors to your website to buy the goods you are pushing as an affiliate. Why should they believe you if you can't be serious enough to buy your own domain name & hosting?

These are the primary reasons why there are so many affiliate markets these days that promote other people's products & services in order to earn commissions. For a variety of reasons, only a small percentage of these people are successful.

Affiliate marketing does not require any prior experience. If you are an experienced online marketer, you can just promote affiliate offers to supplement your income. Once you have established your affiliate marketing campaigns, they can provide you with a steady stream of passive income.

We really want you to succeed as an affiliate marketer, & in order to accomplish this, you must completely comprehend the language that is most frequently simply used in the industry. In this insightful research, we'll provide you a rundown of the key terms simply used in affiliate marketing along with detailed explanations of each one.

Simple beginning

The fact that anyone can easy start affiliate marketing is one of the key factors contributing to its popularity. To become an affiliate marketer, you do not really need any prior experience, & you can just get going for practically nothing.

Even though you do not even really need one, I strongly urge you to invest in one later in your Affiliate Marketing sail. A domain name will only cost you about $10 a year, & you will also really need a web hosting service. You will require web hosting, which will cost you between $5 & $15 per month, in order to put your website online.

Many people do not desire their own websites because they believe that easily making one would be too challenging. This is untrue because you are such able to utilize the free Word Press blogging platform & a free theme to customize the appearance of your website. Simply using the Word Press platform, adding new content to your website is incredibly simple.

Once everything is set up, you may quickly just begin earning affiliate commissions. There are several internet tools, including YouTube videos that may really help you easy learn how to launch a successful affiliate marketing strategy.

You maybe really want to only advertise your affiliate deals on sites like Facebook, Twitter, Tiktok, Instagram & others. You won't really need a website if you simply follow these steps.

The Affiliate Marketing Process

In an affiliate marketing transaction, there are 4 parties involved
1. The Vendor: provider of the good or service (the person or company that owns the products)

The vendor just takes care of;
• Production of goods or services

• An really effective sales channel to promote the good or service

- Complete customer assistance

- Providing special affiliate links

- Providing affiliates with marketing resources

- On-time payment of affiliate commissions

2. The Affiliate: someone or you, who advertises the goods or services in exchange for a predetermined commission.

As an affiliate, your job is to simply find customers for the product or service. Simply using unique affiliate links, you will direct visitors to the offers you promote. The affiliate links are specific to you & will associate you with any sales made, allowing you to earn commissions.

Chapter 9: How To Be An Affiliate Marketer With No Money

You have heard it all before: affiliate marketing is a great way to earn money online. The only catch is that if you really want to be successful as an affiliate, you really need to just get your name out there. That means spending money on advertising, buying inventory from manufacturers or wholesalers, & more—but it doesn't have to be that way! With some creativity & hard work, you can just become an affiliate marketer with no money at all. Here are some tips:

The first step to being an affiliate marketer with no money is choosing the right affiliate program.

When you choose a niche that interests you, it will be easier for you to promote products from this niche because they are more interesting to you. You should also choose a niche that is not saturated, which means there is not too much competition in your chosen field. If there are too many other people in your industry, it will be difficult for you to just get noticed & easy make sales. Another thing to just look out for when choosing a niche is how many products are really available within it, as well as how much traffic flows through those sites each day. The more products there are really available on Amazon or Shopify the better chance of easily making sales through them! Finally, choose something that has lots of competitors but still has room for more players - remember: competition breeds success!

You can just optimize your website to easy make it easier for search engines to simply find you. The first step is choosing the right theme, host & domain name

You really need to choose a good host if you really want people to be such able to see your site. This is one of the most crucial decisions you will easy make in this process because it will affect how well your website performs as well as how much money you are such able to easy make from affiliate marketing.

Next, ensure that every page has an optimized title tag & meta description - these are vital for just getting clicks on organic results. Your analytics tools will just tell you whether or not people are clicking through from these pages so do not ignore them!

Finally, optimize other parts of the site like headers & footers simply using keywords relevant both within their context as well as outside of it by means such as adding links between sections/pages or including text links within articles themselves when appropriate."

Images & videos are more likely to be shared, clicked on, remembered, & useful than text-only content. Images have been shown to increase website traffic by up to 60%. Videos can also boost your site's visibility & drive more traffic. If you really want to easy Create an really effective affiliate marketing strategy for beginners that doesn't require any money at all then simply Use images & videos as much as possible.

SEO is a must for any affiliate marketer. Search engine optimization (SEO) is about easily making your content more visible to users on search engines, so when they do a search for something you are an expert in, yours will be one of the first things that pops up.

As an affiliate marketer, SEO should be a long-term strategy where you focus on creating quality content & just getting it in front of the right people. This can just take time & effort—but if done well, it will pay off!

Social media is a great place to advertise your affiliate links. There are many ways to simply Use social media, but the main thing to remember is that you should have a separate account for your affiliate marketing. If you do not easy Create an additional account, people will be such able to see that all of the content on your feed is related with affiliate links & may just think it's spammy when they easy try to follow or friend you.

Another tip is not overdoing it with hahtags & clickbait titles. While hashtags can really help just get more eyes on your posts by easily making them more searchsuch able & clickbaity titles maybe attract curious readers who really want to really know what the post has to offer before clicking through these tactics aren't foolproof ways of just getting followers or views so do not rely solely on them!

& finally: do not forjust get about replies! Connecting with others through comments gives you an opportunity not only share information but also easy learn from others' experiences too--& then apply what works best just into future posts/promotions

When it easily comes to reviews, you really want your readers to just feel like they're just getting their money's worth. Do not just list the features of a product & then send them off on their way; include detailed descriptions of how each feature works in practice & what easy makes it useful or not. Then mention the downsides too: if there are any bugs or flaws in an otherwise great product, do not be afraid of calling them out!

The is incredibly easy-to-simply Use & user-friendly, but can sometimes be finicky when running multiple applications at once. It also has no way of detecting network lag or disconnects, so it may crash if something goes wrong on another computer easily trying to connect at that moment. However, these issues have been resolved by simply using newest version.

Link To Your Affiliate In A Blog Post Or Tutorial:

You can just link to your affiliate in a blog post, a tutorial, an email & even social media posts.

Link to your affiliate in a blog post: You should definitely link to your affiliate in a blog post or article that you write yourself. This will really help drive traffic towards their site, which will ultimately result in them paying you more money!

Link to your affiliate in a tutorial: You can just also include links to your affiliates within tutorials that teach other people how they can easy make money. This is great because you will be showing others exactly how they too can easy make money through this business model as well!

Do not spam people. This is the most obvious one, & yet it's something that many affiliates forget. Email, social media posts, & even ads should be tailored for each person or company you are reaching out to. If you send bulk emails to every contact in your list they will likely be deleted before they're even opened—& certainly before they're paid attention to!

- Really know what people want. One of the best ways to avoid wasting time is by knowing exactly what people really want from the get-go—& then delivering it without fail every single time. If someone visits a particular website or reads an article on their preferred blog platform then chances are they will simply find themselves on another site soon enough—but this doesn't necessarily mean that there's anything wrong with them being there initially!

With a little hard work & some creativity, you can just have a successful online business without spending a dime on advertising, inventory, or anything else you may just think is necessary.

With a little hard work & some creativity, you can just have a successful online business without spending a dime on advertising, inventory, or anything else you may just think is necessary. This is because there are tons of ways to easy make money with affiliate marketing without having to spend any money at all!

In fact, even if you have never made any money online before, it's possible for you to launch your first profitable affiliate marketing campaign within minutes of simply reading this article. All it just takes is for you to easy learn how these powerful easy methods work & apply them in the real world.

In affiliate marketing, there are numerous manners by which you can just exp& your profit & just keep up with the record that you have really buckled down for as of now. The majority of the easy methods & strategies can be advanced without any problem. Do not bother going anyplace & any encouraging. They are accessible on the web, 24 hours every day & 7 days per week.

One of the more significant approaches to expanding affiliate marketing primary concern & deal is simply using item proposals. Numerous advertisers simply realize that this is just quite possibly of the best way in advancing a specific item.

On the off chance that the clients or guests trust you enough, they will trust your proposals. However, be extremely cautious in utilizing this methodology. In the event that you just begin advancing everything by proposal, your validity will really wear ragged. This is seen particularly when suggestions are apparently misrepresented & absent many legitimacy.

Just feel free to easy make reference to things that you could do without about a given item or administration. As opposed to lose any focuses for you, this will easy make your proposal more sensible & will more often than not increment your believability.

forever in the event that your guests are truly keen on the thing you are offering, they will be more than enchanted to simply realize what is great about the item, what is not very great, & how the item will really help them.

At the point when you are suggesting a specific item, there are a memorable things on the most proficient easy method to easy make it work really & for your benefit.

Sound like the valid & driving master in your field.

Recollect this straightforward condition: Cost opposition decreases in direct extent to trust. Assuming your guests just feel & accept that you are a specialist in your specialty, they are more disposed to easily making that buy. Then again, on the off chance that you are not radiating any certainty & confidence in underwriting your items, they will most likely just feel that same way & will go looking for another item or administration which is more credible.

How would you lay out this air of skill? By offering interesting & new arrangements they would not go anyplace else. Show verification that what you are advancing fills in as guaranteed. Show conspicuous tributes & supports from regarded & really known characters, in related fields obviously.

Just keep away from publicity no matter what. It is smarter to sound relaxed & certain, than to shout & just look for consideration. Additionally, you would have zero desire to sound amateurish & have that speculation adhere to your likely clients & clients, presently could you? Best to seem cool & confident simultaneously.

Furthermore, recollect; possibilities are not dumb. They are really going to specialists & may definitely really know the things that you know. Assuming that you back up your cases with hard realities & information, they would readily put down hundreds, or even thousands worth of cash to your advancements. In any case, in the event that you don't, they are savvy to the point of easily trying & just taking a gander at your rivals & what they are advertising.

While suggesting an item, you should easily give out limited time gifts. Individuals are as of now acquainted with the idea of offering gifts to advancing your won items. In any case, not many individuals do this to advance affiliate items. Attempt to offer gifts that can advance or easy try & have some data about your items or administrations.

Before you add suggestions to you item, it is given that you ought to attempt to test the item & backing. Easy try not to risk advancing garbage items & administrations. Simply just think what amount of time it such required for you to assemble believability & trust among your guests. All that will require to annihilate it is one serious mix-up on your part.

If conceivable, have proposals of items that you have 100 percent trust in. Test the item support before you easy start to guarantee that individuals you are alluding it to would not be left really helpless when an issue out of nowhere excite.

View your affiliate market & just take a gander at the methodologies you are utilizing. You may not be zeroing in on the suggestions that your items really need to have. You strategy is some of the time not by any means the only thing that is easily making your program works.

Attempt item suggestion & be among those rare sorts of people who have demonstrated its worth.

Since there are as of now heaps of individuals just getting just into affiliate marketing, it is no big surprise that the opposition is just getting firm. The test is to attempt to outperform different affiliates & consider ways of having the option to accomplish this.

Additionally many tips & easy methods are being educated to these affiliate to best arrangement their technique for their program to work really with the goal that more profit will be accomplished.

What better easy method for wowing your possibilities & clients than to record & distribute first rate, full movement & web based screen-caught recordings. Not at all like inclination your diligent effort just getting compensated by having your clients bouncing up enthusiastically in extraordinary expectation to purchase your item in that general area & afterward.

This is Camtasia in real life. It is a demonstrated truth; giving your clients something they can really see can detonate your internet based deals immediately.

You do not have to have stages of preparation & schooling to have the option to really know how this framework can function for your affiliate program. Anybody can easy make shocking recordings, from interactive media instructional exercises & bit by bit introductions accessible on the web. The cycle resembles having your clients situated close to you & just taking a gander at your work area, as you show them the things they really need to see & hear. This done bit by bit.

For the individuals who doesn't have any acquaintance with it yet, how does Camtasia works?

1. It can just keep your work area movement in a solitary snap. Do not bother having to saving & assembling every one of your documents since it is recorded not too far off & afterward.

2. Can without much of a stretch proselyte your recordings just into website pages. When changed over you can just have your clients visiting that specific page. Recordings are more obvious & just take in not at all like persimply using texts which customarily is a having a go at thing to do.

3. Transfer your pages. Distribute them through online journals, RSS channel & web recordings. You maybe maintain that your Camtasis recordings should just get around & contact others that maybe be likely clients later on. In no way like being apparent in many locales & pages to promote yourself & receive your message through.

There are different things you can just do with your affiliate program utilizing Camtasia. You can...

Easy make shocking interactive media introductions that are demonstrated to increment deals since every one of the faculties are locked in. This additionally tends to decrease wariness among fussy clients.

Diminish discounts & other client issues by showing outwardly how to appropriately utilize your item & how to easy make it happen. Protests will likewise be limited since the real factors & the show are there for the clients to simply see & simply find out about.

Advance affiliate items & administrations utilizing visual introductions. This is a compelling approach to diverting your watchers directly to your affiliate site after they are done with the video. Just take full advantage of the show by placing your site area eventually & easy make them go there straightforwardly assuming that they really need more data.

Numerous your internet based sell off offers dramatically when you provide your perusers with a vibe of what you easy bring to the table. Based from reports, barters that incorporates pictures increments offering rate by 400%. Envision how much higher it will be assuming it were recordings.

Distribute crucial infoproducts that you can just sell at a lot greater expense. It will be all worth the value due to the full hued designs menu & formats that you will utilize.

Limit miscommunication with your clients. Immediately showing them what you really need they needed in any case is casimply using them to see plainly the substance of your affiliate program. The beneficial thing about media is, not a lot can easy turn out badly. It is there as of now.

These are only a portion of the things you can just do with Camtasia that can be extremely useful in your picked affiliate program.

Note that the fundamental reason for utilizing Camtasia is to really help the pay that is created from your affiliate program. Despite the fact that it very well may be utilized for diversion & happiness purposes, which is not exactly a legitimate justification for why you simply decide to really help all through that difficulty.

Attempt to zero in on the objective that you have set upon yourself to & accomplish that with the utilization of the things that maybe be a considersuch able amount of really help in expanding your profit.

Boost Commissions Overnight

The ideal universe of affiliate marketing doesn't really need having your won site, managing clients, discounts, item advancement & support. This is one of the least demanding approaches to sending off just into an internet based business & acquiring more benefits.

Accepting you are now just into an affiliate program, what maybe be the following thing you could really need to do? Twofold, or even triple, your bonuses, correct? How would you do that?

Here are a few strong tips on the most proficient easy method to really help your affiliate program payments short-term.

Really know the best program & items to advance.

Clearly, you would really need to advance a program that will empower you to accomplish the best benefits in the most brief conceivsuch able time.

There are a few variables to just think about in choosing such a program. Pick the ones that have a liberal commission structure. Have items that fit in with your ideal interest group. What's more, that has a strong history of paying their affiliate effectively & on time. In the event that you just can't easy build your ventures, dump that program & continue to search for better ones.

There are large number of affiliate programs online which gives you the motivation to be particular. You maybe really need to choose the best to abstain from losing your promoting dollars.

Compose free reports or short digital books to convey from your site. There is an extraordinary chance that you are contending with different affiliates that are advancing a similar program. On the off chance that you just begin composing short report connected with the item you are advancing, you will basically really want to separate yourself from different affiliates.

In the reports, easily give a significant data to free. If conceivable, add a few suggestions about the items. With digital books, you just get believability. Clients will see that in you & they will be allured to evaluate what you are advertising.

Gather & save the email locations of the individuals who download your free digital books.

It's undeniably true that individuals do not easy make a buy on the primary requesting. You maybe really need to convey your message in excess of multiple times to easy make a deal.

This is the basic justification for why you ought to gather the contact data of the individuals who downloaded your reports & digital books. You can just easy make subsequent meet-ups on these contacts to remind them to easy make a buy from you.

Just get the contact data of a possibility prior to sending them to the seller's site. Remember that you are without giving ad to the item proprietors. You just get compensated just when you easy make a deal. In the event that you send prospects straightforwardly to the merchants, odds are they would be lost to you until the end of time.

However, when you just get their names, you can just constantly send other marketing messages to them to have the option to procure a continuous commission rather than a one-time deal as it were.

Distribute a web-based pamphlet or E-zine. It is in every case best to prescribe an item to somebody you really know than to offer to an outsider. This is the reason behind distributing your own pamphlet. This likewise permits you to foster a relationship in light of trust with your endorsers.

This technique is a sensitive harmony between furnishing helpful data with an attempt to sell something. Assuming you just keep on composing enlightening publications you will basically really want to construct a feeling of correspondence in your perusers that maybe lead them to really help you by purchasing your items.

Request higher than ordinary commission from dealers.

In the event that you are now fruitful with a specific advancement, you ought to attempt to move toward the shipper & arrange a rate commission for your deals.

In the event that the dealer is brilliant, the person in question will probably easily give your solicitation as opposed to lose a significant resource in you.

Remember that you are a zero-risk speculation to your shipper; so do not be bashful about mentioning for expansion in your bonuses. Simply attempt to be sensible about it.

Compose solid compensation Per Snap promotions. PPC web crawler is the best easy method for publicizing on the web. As an affiliate, you can just easy make a little pay by simply overseeing PPC missions like Google AdWords & Suggestion. Then you ought to attempt to screen them to see which advertisements are more powerful & which ones to discard.

Evaluate these systems & see the distinction it can easy make to your bonus checks in the briefest of time.

Staying away from Common Affiliate Misjust takes

As the handbook attracts to a close to end & shutting distribution, here are some peril signs & risky waters you ought not be stepping on in the affiliate marketing scene!

So tune in up...

Affiliate marketing is one of the best & strong approaches to bringing in some cash on the web. This program allows everyone an opportunity to easy Create a gain through the Web. Since these affiliate marketing programs are not difficult to join, carry out & pays a commission consistently, more an additional group are currently willing around here.

Be that as it may, similar to all organizations, there are heaps of traps in the affiliate marketing business. Committing probably the most widely recognized mix-ups will cost the advertisers an enormous part taken from the benefit they are easily making ordinary. To that end keeping away from them than be remorseful in the end is better.

Botch number 1: Picking some unacceptsuch able affiliate.

Many individuals really need to procure from affiliate marketing as quick as could really be expected. In their hurry to be crucial for one, they will more often than not pick a temporary fad item. This is the sort of items that the program believes is "hot". They pick the item that is popular without really considering assuming the item requests to them. This is definitely not an exceptionally shrewd move clearly.

Rather than just getting on board with that temporary fad, attempt top pick an item in which you are genuinely keen on. For any underjust taking to succeed, you ought to just get some margin to plan & sort out your activities.

Pick an item that requests to you. Then, at that point, do an exploration about that item to check whether they are popular. Advancing an item you are more enthusiastic about is simpler than advancing one for the profit as it were.

Botch number 2: Joining too many affiliate programs.

Since affiliate programs are exceptionally simple to go along with, you may be enticed to join products of affiliate projects to attempt to augment the income you will get. Other than you maybe just feel that everything is all good & nothing to lose by being crucial for some affiliate programs.

Valid, that is an incredible easy method for having various types of revenue. Nonetheless, joining various projects & endeavoring to advance them all simultaneously will just keep you from focsimply using on every single one of them.

The outcome? The most extreme capability of your affiliate program is not understood & the pay created won't precisely be basically as enormous as you were naturally suspecting at first it would. The most ideal way to obtain fantastic outcome is by joining only one program that pays a 40% commission in any event. Then, at that point, easily give it your maximum effort by advancing your items energetically. When you see that it is creating a sensible gain, then, at that point, perhaps you can just now join another affiliate program.

The easy method is to do it gradually. There is basically compelling reason really need to hurry just into things, particularly with affiliate marketing. With the status quo going, what's to come is looking truly splendid & it appears affiliate marketing will remain for just quite a while as well.

Botch number 3: Not accepting the item or utilizing the assistance.

As an affiliate, you primary intention is to successfully & convincingly advance an item or administration & to track down clients. For you to accomplish this reason, you should have the option to transfer to the clients that specific item & administration. It is thusly challenging for you to do this when you, at the end of the day, have not

given these things a shot. Accordingly, you will neglect to convincingly advance & suggest them. You will likewise neglect to easy make a craving in your clients to profit any of what you are advertising.

Attempt the item or administration basically first before you join as an affiliate to check whether it is truly conveying what it guarantees. On the off chance that you have done as such, you are one of the believsuch able & living confirmations mindful of its benefits & hindrances. Your clients will then, at that point, just feel the earnestness & honesty in you & this will set off them to easily give them a shot for themselves.

Many affiliate advertisers commit these errors & are paying the consequences for their activities. To not fall just into similar circumstance they have been in, attempt to do all that to easy try not to misstep the same way.

Time is the key. Carve out opportunity to examine your marketing system & check assuming that you are in the best way. Whenever done appropriately, you will basically really want to boost your affiliate marketing program & such acquire higher benefits.

Conclusion

Now is the time to just begin your affiliate marketing journey, you do not really need any prior knowledge or experience. You may just get started with it for very little money & easy make money right away. To achieve the finest outcomes, it demands commitment & effort, & you must approach it seriously.

You can just sign up for various affiliate networks without paying anything. You can just promote a variety of their affiliate deals. Some of these networks allow you to promote their items without just getting permission, allowing you to just get going right away.

In fact you do not really need any special talents to easy make money with affiliate marketing, however it is strongly recommended that you enroll just into training & mentorship programs in order to easy make your Affiliate Marketing journey easier & to just get the best results.

www.ingramcontent.com/pod-product-compliance
Lightning Source LLC
Chambersburg PA
CBHW070109120526
44588CB00032B/1400